1/N/08

S0-ATV-252

Bookcloth in
England and America
1823–50

Bookcloth in England and America
1823–50

Andrea Krupp

Oak Knoll Press
The British Library
The Bibliographical Society of America
2008

First Edition 2008

Published by:

Oak Knoll Press
310 Delaware Street
New Castle, DE 19702

The British Library
96 Euston Road
London NW1 2DB

The Bibliographical Society of America
P.O. Box 1537, Lenox Hill Station
New York, NY 10021

Copyright © The Bibliographical Society of America, 2008
All rights reserved

ISBN: 978-1-58456-213-9 (Oak Knoll Press)
ISBN: 978-0-7123-5007-5 (The British Library)

Publishing Director: Mark S. Parker Miller
Typesetting: Laura R. Williams

A previous version of this work was published as
"Bookcloth in England and America, 1823-50," *The Papers of the
Bibliographical Society of America* 100:1 (2006): 25-87.

No part of this book may be reproduced in any manner without the
express written consent of the publisher, except in cases of brief excerpts
in critical reviews and articles. All inquiries should be addressed to:
Oak Knoll Press, 310 Delaware Street, New Castle, DE 19720.

Printed in China on acid-free paper meeting the requirements
of ANSI/NISO Z39.48-1992 (Permanance of Paper)

Cataloging-in-Publication data available from the publishers

E
69.3
.S8
78
2008

Contents

Preface

When I was starting in the field, a man more advanced than I mentioned that cloth grains speak to you from across the room. I was taken aback—they were not conversing with me. If they could speak, I was unable to hear them. I went on to learn, from reading contemporary accounts, that graining was a process of "imprinting all over the cloth, of a small and uniform pattern calculated to hide the barrenness and stiff uniformity of the threads in the cloth." Graining persisted for sixty years through a succession of patterns, each usually quite limited in time.

By 1890, a natural look was in favor for bookcloth. One critic wrote dismissively that cloths "with arbitrary grains" were no longer wanted. Grainings went out of fashion and are not seen on bookcloths today. But they remain on the nineteenth-century books—the plentiful brown rib grains, the rare pansy-face grains, the often amazing beauty of the ribbon-embossed patterns.

The grains are important. Not only can we date bindings by a knowledge of grain development, but they are also an essential part of our tactile and visual experience of the book covers. They are historical, unique, uncopyable. They excite our wonder and curiosity. Such recent scholars as Blanck, Tanselle, and Ball have carried their study forward and offered models for naming and description, with a selection of pictured representations.

In the history of the mechanization of cotton spinning and weaving (1780-1820), several names stand out—Kay's flying shuttle, Hargreaves's spinning jenny. A good portion of inventive England seemed absorbed in solving problems of individual parts. Then came Richard Arkwright, gifted with the ability to see the whole, how to put the parts together in sequence to produce machine-made cotton.

In her own field, Andrea Krupp has accomplished something of what Sir Richard Arkwright did in his. Taking the beginnings of others, building on them with discipline and scholarship, she has created a working system of cloth grain nomenclature and identification.

Advances in photographic reproduction allow the showing of a picture of every grain, referenced by name and number. To me the most valuable feature is the precise date span assigned to each grain—provisionally, since this is a system destined to expand.

Now, in truth, cloth grains speak a language—a language we can all learn to read. Andrea's book provides its dictionary and grammar—concise, handy, indispensable. It would be impossible to embark on any consideration of cloth grains without it.

Sue Allen

Acknowledgements

I would like to acknowledge the support and assistance of my friends and colleagues at the Library Company. From the very beginning of this project, Chief of Conservation Jennifer W. Rosner has been a close collaborator. Her organized mind shaped the Database of 19th-Century Cloth Bindings, from which my data for this research and the Catalogue of 19th-Century Bookcloth Grains was drawn. Her dogged persistence over a span of twelve years gave the momentum to this very large, ambitious project, and thanks to her efforts, the Database is finally in the last stages of preparation for mounting online. Curator of Printed Books Wendy Woloson provided invaluable help with her skillful editing. Also, with her sharp eyes and curator's purse she enthusiastically helped to build the Library Company's collection of 19th-century cloth bindings. Early on, Librarian Jim Green recognized the potential utility of my research and offered unwavering support along the way, and I credit Director John Van Horne for fostering a work environment that values staff involvement with the collections. Sharon Hildebrand and Linda Wisniewski provided expertise in scanning the grain patterns, and Jenny Ambrose continues to be a key resource for navigating the technological intricacies of mounting the Database of 19th-Century Cloth Bindings, and soon, the Catalogue of 19th-Century Bookcloth Grains online. Thank you to all of my colleagues in the McLean Conservation Department: Alice Austin and Kristin Balmer, as well as the rest of the staff of the Library Company in the Cataloging Department, the Print and Photograph Department, the reading room, and administration. Special thanks to Michael Zinman, head cheerleader of this project from its inception. He has been an important contributor intellectually, materially, and financially.

The compilation of grain patterns in the CBG was a group effort, and I thank all the contributors whose sharp eyes and minds have enriched my work. Todd Pattison, Willman Spawn, Sue Allen, Steve Beare, Tom Kinsella, and Robert Milevski provided not only contributions of patterns but also intellectual exchange. Todd Pattison contributed four new patterns: Dia14, Ft44, As14 and Gs3. Stuart Walker of the Boston Public Library made a significant contribution of fourteen new patterns. As13, Fs18, Fs19, Fs20, Ft41, Ft42, Ft43, Ft47, Gs1, Gs2, Gt20, Gt21, Gt22 and Gt23 appear courtesy of the Boston Public Library, and I thank them for providing scans of these patterns. Ft29 appears courtesy of the Athenaeum of Philadelphia. At17 and As15 appear courtesy of Steve Beare. I gleaned two patterns from the Publishers' Bindings Online website: Ft45 and Ft46; these images appear courtesy of the W.S. Hoole Special Collections Library at the University of Alabama.

Bookcloth in England and America, 1823–50

PART 1: EARLY BOOKCLOTH

IN 1823, a London bookbinder named Archibald Leighton collaborated with a dyer to transform plain cotton fabric into a material suited to the covering of books.[1] Bookcloth, as it came to be known, was easy to work with, easy to decorate, and much cheaper than leather. The new binding material soon revolutionized bookbinding—both the process and the product—in England and America. Book historians such as Michael Sadleir, John Carter, Joseph Rogers, Douglas Ball, and most recently William Tomlinson and Richard Masters have told this story of invention.[2] However, the history of the early period of bookcloth, from the first experiments up to the time when manufacturers perfected the product and launched an industry, from 1823 to about 1850, remains frustratingly obscure.

Little is known about how, where, and by whom early bookcloth was produced. Primary source material that would provide documentary evidence about the manufacture and use of bookcloth during the first decades of its existence, such as advertisements, patents, and publishers' and binders' records, remains scarce.[3] However, cloth-bound books

1 Douglas Leighton, "Canvas and Bookcloth: An Essay on Beginnings," *The Library*, 5th ser., 3 (June 1948): 39-49.

2 Michael Sadleir, *The Evolution of Publishers' Binding Styles, 1770–1900* (London: Constable; New York: R. R. Smith, 1930); John Carter, *Binding Variants* (London: Constable and Company, 1932); Joseph W. Rogers, "The Rise of American Edition Binding" in *Bookbinding in America*, ed. H. Lehmann-Haupt (New York: R. R. Bowker, 1941); Douglas Ball, *Victorian Publishers' Bindings* (Williamsburg, VA: Bookpress, 1985); William Tomlinson and Richard Masters, *Bookcloth, 1823–1980* (Mellor, Stockport, Cheshire: Dorothy Tomlinson, 1996)

3 Some of the earliest U.S. patents exist only as subject entries in an index, the

themselves are a rich source of empirical information, and repositories such as the Library Company of Philadelphia hold them in plentiful supply. Since 1995, the Library Company's Chief of Conservation, Jennifer Woods Rosner, and I have been compiling data about the structure and appearance of cloth-covered bindings in our collection. The Database of Nineteenth-century Cloth Bindings currently contains data on approximately 3,000 books published between 1824 and 1900. Each entry comprises over sixty fields of information that record the details of the book's structure and appearance. This article focuses on two of those recorded elements: the date of publication as given on the title-page and the grain of the cloth. While compiling the database we identified 160 new bookcloth grain patterns. The majority of them, 135, first appear on American books published before 1850.[4] By way of comparison, current resources illustrate fifty-seven different bookcloth grains,[5] and only seventeen of them are pre-1850 patterns.

The study of nineteenth-century bookbindings is advancing with increased attention to the materiality of the book and the information that can be gleaned from it, because documentary evidence is so rare. Accordingly, the study of bookcloth grain patterns by necessity must progress towards increasingly detailed and specific identification and away from generalized divisions of grain patterns by family. The large number of bookcloth grains that has been amassed underscores the need for a detailed and accurate "field guide" that records individual cloth grain pat-

---

actual patents having burned in the great Patent Office fire of 15 December 1836. Three of these were especially promising: a ribbon smoothing and glossing machine, 1817; cloth dressing and ornamenting, 1821; manufacture of figured fabrics, 1834.

4 Both totals include 104 "ribbon-embossed" patterns. These decorative bookcloth grain patterns in floral, geometric, and abstract designs are discussed later in this article. Their dates of use range from the early to mid-1830s through the 1840s.

5 Photographs of cloth grains appear in the following books: Sadleir, *The Evolution of Publishers' Binding Styles;* Carter, *Binding Variants*; Rogers, "The Rise of American Edition Binding"; Sadleir, *XIX Century Fiction: A Bibliographical Record Based on His Own Collection*, 2 vols. (London: Constable; Berkeley, CA: California Univ. Press, 1951; reprinted, 1969); Jacob Blanck and Michael Winship, *Bibliography of American Literature*, 9 vols. (New Haven, CT: Yale Univ. Press, 1955–91); G. Thomas Tanselle, "The Bibliographical Description of Patterns," *Studies in Bibliography* 23 (1970): 71–102; Philip Gaskell, *A New Introduction to Bibliography* (Oxford: Clarendon, 1972); Ball, *Victorian Publishers' Bindings.*

terns. For example, current resources illustrate two rib grains, but we have identified ten different rib grains, each with a quantifiable distinguishing characteristic. Furthermore, each one is associated with a limited range of dates, and eight of these rib-grain patterns first appear before 1850. Acute diagonal rib (rib9) is an example of a highly individual, easily recognizable, and potentially significant early rib-grain pattern. I have recorded nine examples of acute diagonal rib at the Library Company, and all date from 1832 to 1837. Though rare, examples of this unique grain will seem to pop off the shelf once your eyes have learned to spot it.

In all, 247 grain patterns[6] have been assembled to create a new "field guide" for identifying and dating nineteenth-century bookcloth. The Catalogue of Nineteenth-century Bookcloth Grains (CBG) appears in its entirety at the end of this article. The existing "descriptive" nomenclature of cloth grains provided a model for naming new patterns that was followed whenever possible.[7] It is important to remember that the data presented in the CBG is drawn primarily from the Database of Nineteenth-century Cloth Bindings. Approximately one-quarter of the cloth bindings in the Library Company of Philadelphia's collection of predominantly pre-1860 American imprints has been entered into the database to date. Seventy-one percent of the new grain patterns appear on American books printed before 1850, which may be partly due to the strong representation in our collection, and accordingly, the database, of pre-1860 imprints. But I believe that the diversity of cloth-grain patterns extant before 1850 is in itself an important and previously unrecognized aspect of the early history of bookcloth manufacture. Beyond amassing cloth grain varieties, the CBG records the dates of use for each grain as recorded in the Database of Nineteenth-century Cloth Bindings.[8] Larger pools of data for both English and American imprints must be

6   This total includes 25 new patterns added to the CBG since the first printing of this article.

7   Part 2 of this article addresses the issues of nomenclature and descriptive vs. code-based systems of identification.

8   Bearing in mind the publishers' practice of binding up parts of an edition sometimes many years after its initial publication, the dating of a particular bookcloth grain based solely upon the year of imprint can be unreliable. However, after examining thousands of examples of nineteenth-century cloth-bound books, one develops an eye for the "solitary exception," as Carter put it, and the discipline to regard it with suspicion.

compiled and tallied before "first appearance" dates can be established with any certainty, but this important component of the catalogue will continue to be refined as research continues. Even as it evolves, I hope that the CBG will facilitate other data-gathering projects similar to ours, as well as provide a resource to support the preservation and appreciation of nineteenth-century cloth bindings.

The large variety of early bookcloth grain patterns found on American books (and presumably English books as well) points to a fruitful collaboration between bookbinders and textile workers. Cloth finishers, dyers, and calenderers, using tools and processes that had been in use since the late fifteenth century, possessed the machinery and the knowledge required to make bookcloth.[9] Some bookbinders, like Archibald Leighton, by necessity made their own bookcloth until it became commercially available,[10] but it was the textile finishers, with their rolling presses and their expertise, who provided the foundation that future bookcloth manufacturers built on.

The existence of "moiré"[11] patterns among the earliest bookcloth grains is evidence of the close link between the cloth-finishing trades and early bookcloth manufacture. The calenderer[12] used a rolling machine to apply friction, pressure, and sometimes heat to the surface of a fabric

9   Under the entry for *Calender*, contemporary British government documents from 1513 reference the "calandring of Worsted." Even earlier, under the entry for *Calenderer*, is a 1495 reference to "calenderars of the same Worstedis" (*OED*)

Florence M. Montgomery, *Textiles in America, 1650–1870* (New York: W. W. Norton and Company, 1984), 231, 256. The entry for "Embossing" cites a pamphlet written in 1716 that mentions "flower'd imboss'd cloth." The entry for "Harateen" describes a cloth made in 1750 embossed with a "wavy pattern here achieved by means of a hot copper cylinder."

10   Tomlinson and Masters, 14.

11   Also called "watered." A moiré pattern is an optical effect, created by superimposing two sets of parallel lines, or grids. This effect can be observed by placing two layers of fine mesh screen or fabric one atop the other, slightly out of alignment.

12   *A General Description of All Trades, Digested in Alphabetical Order* (London: T. Waller, 1747) describes the calenderer as one who is "the Finisher(s) of divers Linnen, Woolen, and Silk Goods in the Piece for the shop-keepers by rolling, with a great Weight…to render them smooth, compact and glossy " (50). In *The New and Complete Dictionary of Arts and Sciences* (London: 1763), the entry for calender describes a machine weighted with 20,000 lbs. of stones, which applied pressure to the cloth being "watered" (436).

making it compressed and smooth and giving the surface a variety of finishes such as plain, moiré, and embossed.[13] The 1839 *Book of Trades* describes one method of creating a moiré pattern and makes reference to a new variety of client, the bookbinder: "That waved appearance often observable on one side of a silk ribband, *and on the cotton cloth, now much employed in bookbinding*, is produced by running two pieces of cloth together between the hot iron and the paper bowl [roller] of a calender. The surfaces of the cloth which face each other are those which become watered."[14] Tomlinson notes that while John Carter considers morocco the first bookcloth grain, two other sources maintain that moiré, or watered, was the first bookcloth grain.[15] In the Library Company's collection, the first appearance date for fine straight grain morocco (lea6) is 1831, and true moiré (moi1) first appears in 1829.[16]

The calenderer also produced a variety of decorative fabrics embossed with elaborate floral, geometric, and abstract designs. Like the moiré finish, they were intended for use in the home and fashion. Bookbinders of the 1830s saw these so-called "ribbon-embossed"[17] patterns as a ready source of decorative designs for bookcloth. A large number of ribbon-embossed patterns have been identified: 107 at the Library Company alone, 92 with dates from 1831 to 1840. After 1840, the use of such highly textural and/or large-scale designs declined sharply, and the number of smooth-surfaced, small-scale patterns increased in variety and popularity. Book historian Michael Sadleir observes this trend and speculates that

13   George S. Cole, *Encyclopedia of Dry Goods: A Reference Book for the Wholesale and Retail Dry Goods Trade of the United States* (New York: Root Newspaper Association, 1900), lists the following types of calender finishes: dull, luster, glazed, watered or moiré, and embossed (59).

14   *The Book of Trades; or, Circle of the Useful Arts* (Glasgow: Richard Griffen, 1839), 223–4. Italics added.

15   Tomlinson and Masters, 137 n. 20.

16   Carter, 57. Carter states that Heath introduced silk-moiré bindings in 1828. The Library Company has three silk-moiré bindings from 1829 and 1830, but they are not examples of bookcloth, which is made of cotton or linen.

17   Tomlinson and Masters, 14. Though we now associate the term "ribbon" with narrow strips of cloth, ribbon-embossed cloths ranged in width from fourteen to thirty-six inches wide. Tomlinson quotes Robert Leighton as recalling that in 1836, the embossed bookcloth produced on the premises of his father's shop used engraved rollers that were fourteen or fifteen inches wide.

the high cost made bookbinders abandon ribbon-embossed cloth in favor of simpler patterns.[18] Variations of diaper, rib, and moiré, as well as patterns imitating leather, soon replaced ribbon-embossed cloths altogether. The Database of Nineteenth-century Cloth Bindings clearly shows this evolution. Of the books recorded for the year 1834, only 5 percent were covered in ribbon-embossed cloth. In 1835, the number rises dramatically to 56 percent and then gradually declines to 5 percent in 1844. At the same time the number of "regular" grain patterns grew from 20 to 45.

Meanwhile, back in the bindery, the stamping of titles and designs, both in gold and in "blind,"[19] onto the preassembled, bookcloth-covered case was becoming standard practice. It is possible that the texture and pattern of ribbon-embossed cloth interfered, both mechanically and visually, with the stamped titles and designs, and this hastened the evolution towards smoother, simpler grain patterns.

Other styles of bookcloth appeared during this early period (1823– 50), but most were short-lived experiments. "Pre-ornamented" bookcloth, embossed with designs for the front and back covers and the spine before being attached to the boards, typifies this spirit of invention.[20] In a similar vein are examples of cloths with jacquard-woven patterns that embellish both boards and spine, with the title woven in.[21] A simpler variant on ornamenting the bookcloth before application to the boards was employed by The Harper's Family Library series, which appeared throughout the 1830s and '40s. Rules and type were printed in black ink on smooth tan bookcloth.[22] Printed cloth, probably intended for dressmakers or for use in the home, was adapted for bookbinding through starching and calendering. These early printed bookcloths exist in two main styles. The first style appeared in the early 1830s to around 1840 and was characterized by a smooth, glossy, ungrained surface. The palette was gener-

18   Michael Sadleir, *The Evolution of Publishers' Binding Styles,* 47–8.

19   A "blind stamp" is a pattern stamped without gold foil, leaving just an impression.

20   For an in depth discussion of pre-ornamented bookcloth see Andrea Krupp and Jennifer Woods Rosner, "Pre-Ornamented Bookcloth on Nineteenth-century Cloth Case Bindings," *PBSA* 94, no. 2 (2000): 177–96.

21   *The Art of Publishers' Bookbindings, 1815–1915* (Los Angeles: William Dailey Rare Books, 2000), nos. 108, 148.

22   Ibid., nos. 27, 12.

ally earthy and somber, and the patterns ranged from naturalistic, organic forms to engine-turned patterns (Illus. 1). The second style appeared in the mid-1840s. These were typically striped patterns in a palette of bright colors, but small scale "calico" type designs, often in green and black, were also used. These cloths were usually grained in a rib or other fine texture. Further embellished with blind and gold stamping, these decorative bindings created a brilliant effect (Illus. 2). By mid-century these charming and inventive approaches to embellishing bookcloth one by one fell by the wayside as the bookcloth manufacture evolved into an industry that naturally emphasized consistency, simplification, and standardization.

The demand for bookcloth became so great that some linen drapers, mercers, dyers, and ribbon embossers began to specialize in bookcloth manufacturing. The cloth finishing industry was already well established in both England and America by the 1840s, providing a strong infrastructure for the nascent bookcloth industry. *A Register of the New York Book Trades, 1821–1842* records twelve cloth finishers and fifty-nine cloth dyers,[23] and an 1840 Philadelphia census lists thirty cloth-finishing firms. Naturally, the shift towards specialization began in London, where bookcloth was invented. The first documentary evidence of this shift appeared in an 1840 London *Publishers' Circular* ad for Thomas Hughes, a dyer and calenderer who began to advertise as a "manufacturer of Book-Binding Cloth."[24] By 1844, Ford and Brocklehurst, the sole entry for "Bookbinders' Cloth" in a British business directory three years earlier, were joined by Thomas Hughes, mentioned above, and J.L. Wilson, who was also previously a linen draper.[25]

From thereon, Britain's bookcloth industry kept growing. J.L. Wilson Jr., one of the earliest bookcloth suppliers in London, established two factories in the northeast part of the city around 1847. Until 1868, Wilson was the leading manufacturer of bookcloth in England and a major exporter to the United States.[26] England was soon established as a world leader in the bookcloth manufacturing industry.

23   *A Register of the New York Book Trades, 1821–1842* compiled by Sidney F. and Elizabeth Stege Huttner (New York: The Bibliographical Society of America, 1993).

24   *Publishers' Circular* 3, no. 7 (1840): 269.

25   Tomlinson and Masters, 15.

26   Ibid., 15.

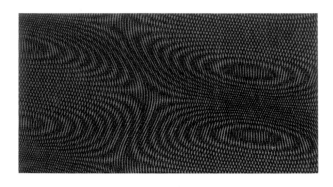

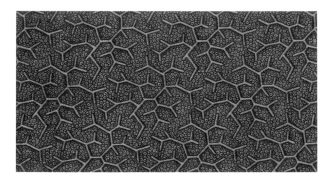

Illus. 1: All of these examples of early printed bookcloth are finished with a smooth glazed surface. *Top:* An engine-turned pattern printed in purple, London, 1833; *Middle:* Organic forms printed in three colors of brown, New York, 1835; *Bottom:* Abstract pattern printed in brown, Baltimore, 1839.

Illus. 2: Two examples of mid-century printed bookcloths: *Top:* Green and black "calico" design with a fine rib grain (rib2), New York, 1847; *Bottom:* Light green and dark green striped design with a fine rib grain (rib2), Philadelphia, 1848.

By comparison, documentary evidence of American bookcloth manufacture is scarce. In his influential essay "The Rise of Edition Binding
in America," Joseph Rogers identifies three sources of American made
bookcloth. Yet he concludes his essay stating "English cloth was used as
a rule from the beginning of the 1820s until the founding of Interlaken
in 1883."[27] Rogers acknowledges the existence of Abbot and Wilcomb,
the first bookcloth manufacturer to be listed in a New York directory,[28]
in 1844. He notes that in 1840 John C. Copper owned a bookbinders'
supply house that sold American made bookcloth.[29] Rogers also mentions the New York Dyeing and Printing Establishment, a cloth finishing
company that expanded into bookcloth manufacture "sometime prior to
1877."[30] In addition, Rogers quotes the treasurer of the American bookcloth manufacturer Interlaken Mills, stating that "Interlaken was the
fourteenth American concern to 'dabble' in the making of bookcloth."[31] I
have found two new references to bookcloth manufacturing in America.
Edwin T. Freedley, in his book on American industry in 1856, mentions
E. D. Marshall and Company, a Philadelphia firm that "engraved cyl-
inders for…embossing paper hangings and bookbinder's muslin."[32] And
two years later, the same author writes of N. M. Abbot and Company, a
New York bookcloth manufacturer, "This house is entitled to very great
credit for their successful and persevering efforts to produce an article of
American manufacture fully equal in all respects to the imported, and
cheaper. *Their sales now exceed one half the entire present importation.*"[33]
However interesting, documentary evidence of early American bookcloth

27   Rogers, 167.

28   Ibid., 164.

29   Ibid., 162. Stated in a letter to Joseph Rogers by a subsequent owner of the firm,
Owen Shoemaker.

30   Ibid., 164-5.

31   Ibid., 164.

32   Edwin T. Freedley, *Leading Pursuits and Leading Men* (Philadelphia: Edward
Young, 1856), 231.

33   Edwin T. Freedley, *Philadelphia and Its Manufactures* (Philadelphia: Edward
Young, 1858), 178, italics added. Freedley goes on to say that "the trade would find an
advantage in using the American in preference to the foreign article. This volume
we shall order to be bound in American muslin."

manufacture is admittedly meager. Until additional documentation is discovered, we must focus our attention on gathering empirical evidence from books that were printed and bound in nineteenth-century America.

It is clear that American bookcloth manufacture, less a seamless history than a sporadic series of attempts, never threatened British dominance in any serious way. Even the relatively successful New York firm of N. M. Abbot and Company eventually yielded sometime after 1858, unable to compete with the flood of bookcloth exported by Wilson and Bentley from England.[34] Yet as evidenced by the large number of early bookcloth grain patterns in the collection at the Library Company, the domestic bookcloth industry, however short-lived or small in scale, probably made a significant contribution to the wide variety of early bookcloth grain patterns that have been discovered. Pinpointing the date of first appearance and duration of use for the earliest bookcloth grain patterns, those produced on a small scale for local consumption, is our key to understanding the fascinating and largely undocumented period of preindustrial bookcloth manufacture both in England and America.

With a large pool of data on bookcloth grains at our fingertips, it is useful and interesting to revisit Joseph Rogers's conclusions about bookcloth manufacture in America. Rogers constructs his arguments on facts gleaned from John Carter's prose outline of the progression of grain patterns in England in *Binding Variants, 1820–1900*. Carter's reference images of bookcloth grain patterns provide a basis for Roger's survey of equivalent patterns on American imprints. Setting out his comparisons in a table, Rogers remarks of British bookcloth "several distinct bookcloth styles [were] prevalent before 1840, which would indicate that production was going forward on a sufficiently large scale to permit the exportation of sizable quantities to America." Continuing this line of reasoning, Rogers compares Carter's roughly estimated first appearance dates for eleven bookcloth grain patterns with the results of his (presumably) small study of American equivalents. Observing a lag time of several years in most cases, Rogers infers that "…England was the chief source of the bookcloth used in America during these early years."[35]

In contrast to his first point, 137 grain patterns have been identified on American imprints with a first appearance date not later than 1840,

34   Rogers, 167.

35   Ibid., 160.

a fact that puts Rogers's reasoning, based on "several distinct book cloth styles," on shaky ground. As for the second part of his argument, when the Library Company equivalents for Carter's eleven grain patterns are taken into account, the majority of first appearance dates are pushed back, in some cases even earlier than the dates established by Carter for British imprints, further undermining Rogers's conclusion.[36] One hundred sixty-one bookcloth grain patterns have been counted on American books published between 1831 and 1847, the period *before* bookcloth was known to be exported in large quantity by a British manufacturer.[37] Many of the grain patterns discovered at the Library Company are rare, seen on fewer than five books. By virtue of their uniqueness, these early grains, especially those that show evidence of a hand-engraved pattern (Illus. 3), may one day allow us to associate a particular bookcloth grain with a publisher or binder and track its use and distribution. Of course, many questions remain unanswered: how much (or how little) book-cloth was produced in America? which early bookcloth grains are orig-inal American designs? and why did bookcloth manufacturing never grow into an important industry in America? As research continues, contributions of data from a variety of sources, especially from British collections, will help to answer these questions and provide a clearer understanding of early nineteenth-century bookcloth, its manufacture, and its stylistic evolution.

My interest in the topic of nineteenth-century cloth bindings grew out of my work as a conservator—observing the qualities that set these books apart from others in our collection and responding to the unique nature of the materials and structures of these bindings. My printmak-ing background provides me a practical understanding of the processes used to create and reproduce designs, for example, to understand the

36 The reference photographs provided by Carter and Rogers appear without a scale, and the reproductions are of varying quality, making positive identification for some of the grains difficult. Also Rogers's and Carter's *ripple* and *embossed* appear to be entirely different grain patterns. After matching CBG patterns to Carter's illustrations, the first appearance dates (Library Company, then Rogers) are as fol-lows: (mo11) 1829, (c) 1832; (dia3) 1835, (d) 1835; (as6) 1837, (e) 1837; (rib3) 1836, (f) 1839; (wav3) 1847, (g) 1846; (wav5) 1847, (h) 1860; (bea5) 1845, (i) 1858; (san1) 1850, (k) 1865; (ban7) 1862, (l) 1865.

37 Tomlinson and Masters, 15. Wilson and Bentley was the largest exporter from 1847 until 1868, when Winterbottom products predominated.

difference between a stamped and an embossed design.[38] The Database of Nineteenth-century Cloth Bindings and the CBG evolved as Jennifer Rosner and I saw an opportunity to record information about the changing structures and materials that we were handling in the course of our work.[39] Along with new binding materials such as bookcloth, the early nineteenth-century bindery was transformed by the introduction of assembly line methods. A bookbinder plying his trade during this period would have witnessed the introduction of assembly line methods and increasingly complicated machinery. The volumes that were produced during the early period of this transition are of particular interest; they speak to us of the bookbinder's struggle to adapt to new materials and new workflow, the pressure to work faster in order to keep up with the machines, and all of these concerns are vividly conveyed through the book's materiality.

Part 2: Bookcloth Grain Nomenclature

Data-gathering studies such as ours (there are likely similar projects ongoing in both England and America) are bound to enrich our understanding of the history of early nineteenth-century bookcloth. Many new cloth grain patterns have already been found, but they must be identified using a consistent set of standards, such as a name or a code, and be keyed to an accurate, scaled image. The identification of bookcloth grain patterns can be approached in two ways, described by John Carter as "roughly descriptive" and "severely technical."[40] Carter opts for a descriptive approach, using some of Sadleir's terms such as "ripple-grain," "sand grain," and "dot-and-line."[41] Philip Gaskell's and Douglas Ball's later work on cloth grain nomenclature also used descriptive terminology. Using a different approach, the editors of the *Bibliography of American Literature* and G. Thomas Tanselle apply letter and number

---

38   For a discussion of stamping and embossing see Krupp and Rosner, "Pre-Ornamented Bookcloth," 179.

39   The majority of our collections are organized chronologically, providing a unique opportunity to study the evolution of cloth binding styles.

40   Carter, xvi.

41   Ibid., xvii.

codes. William Tomlinson, having spent a lifetime working in the book-cloth manufacturing industry, holds out the Winterbottom code system as a model for cloth grain identification.

The CBG employs a descriptive approach to grain identification that follows the vocabulary set by Sadleir, Carter, Gaskell, and Ball. In earlier versions of the CBG we considered following Tanselle's three-digit code system, but it proved to be too rigid to accommodate the expanding families of grains. The letter codes introduced by the Winterbottom Book Cloth Company were also considered. After researching the Tomlinson Collection and evaluating the Winterbottom system of letter codes, I found several problems with this method.[42] First, the Winterbottom circular and subsequent swatch books list only those grains that were currently available, predominantly from 1870 and on. In all, only fifty-four designs are coded,[43] falling far short of the requirements of a catalogue of this scope. Second, while some of the earliest grain patterns such as rib, morocco, diaper, and moiré appear throughout the entire nineteenth century in many variations, the Winterbottom equivalents of these grains represent late nineteenth-century versions of these patterns. While the Winterbottom version shares some similarities with its predecessor, it is clear that they are not the same grain. For example, ultra fine diagonal rib (rib5) is a rare bookcloth grain that is unique to the 1840s. Though at first glance it appears similar to Winterbottom's "S" grain (rib10), a very common grain that came into use in the 1870s, the line count is different. Similarly, it would diminish the significance of early scallop tile (mis5) to equate it to Winterbottom's PP (win3). Using a late nineteenth-century system to describe the earliest book-cloth grain patterns places undue emphasis on the ultimate evolution of the patterns and to my mind detracts from the significance of the primary forms.

Winterbottom codes, fittingly, identify late nineteenth-century grains that are represented in the swatchbooks. Fifteen positively identified

42   The William Tomlinson Book Cloth Collection, comprised of original documents such as pattern books, advertisements, and memos, now resides at Bryn Mawr College in Pennsylvania, and it is a valuable resource for the study of late nineteenth-century grain patterns. The collection is discussed in an article by Willman Spawn and Thomas E. Kinsella, "The Description of Bookcloth: Making a Case for More Precision," *PBSA* 96, no. 3 (2002): 341–9.

43   Based on a survey of Tomlinson Collection materials.

Winterbottom patterns are included in the catalogue. Some of these have only been found on early twentieth-century imprints,[44] and the whorl (PR & LR) and lizard skin (LS) patterns have not been found in the collection at the Library Company at all, but because they have been previously published in important reference works, they have all been included. In the catalogue that follows, where a late nineteenth-century grain matches one that is illustrated in a Winterbottom swatchbook or circular, its code has been listed on the table. In the case of large grain families such as morocco and diaper that exist in seemingly infinite variations throughout the nineteenth century, I have refrained from listing a Winterbottom code.

A discussion of bookcloth grain nomenclature must also include the term "ribbon-embossed cloth." Ribbon-embossed cloth was popular from the 1830s until the mid-40s when it was abandoned for less elaborate patterns. Michael Sadleir uses the term "ribbon-embossed" in 1930 to describe the fancy grained cloths that were produced at the ribbon-embosser's shop, which bookbinders, along with dressmakers and milliners, purchased and adapted for their own use. In this historical sense, the term would best describe patterns produced before 1841, by which time bookcloth manufacture began to be recognized as a trade of its own. A broader use of the term "ribbon-embossed" describes the appearance, rather than the manufacture, of the cloth. This usage allows for the inclusion of a few later patterns, even up to 1859, which have the decorative floral, geometric, or abstract appearance of ribbon-embossed cloth, but were likely produced by a bookcloth manufacturer. I have opted for the latter usage for two reasons: Douglas Ball uses the term this way,[45] and lack of documentary evidence makes it impossible to establish with certainty by whom, or in what kind of workroom, these bookcloths were produced. Left with the appearance of the cloths as the only guide, I propose the following, admittedly subjective, definition. The term *ribbon-embossed bookcloth* should encompass all bookcloth grains that are floral, geometric, or abstract in design, with a pattern larger than 6 mm. per repeat.

---

44   Tomlinson and Masters, 111. Tomlinson notes that the Winterbottom Company began to sell embossed linen (AR) between 1930 and 1948.

45   "The height of the vogue for ribbon embossing was 1834–8, but examples of later date, 1842–59, have been seen" (Ball, 25).

These beautiful designs, in all their many variations, represent a significant trend in the evolution of bookcloth grain patterns. That said, I feel that the term "ribbon-embossed" is a potentially misleading distinction, and an argument could be made to drop the term entirely. They are, after all, patterns that were created using the same techniques and materials as "regular" grained bookcloth. Although in the CBG that follows, I have roughly sorted ribbon-embossed patterns into five broad categories, another option would be to give each pattern a name (or a code) and integrate them fully into one large table. I have neither attempted to name nor pinpoint dates of use for the 126 ribbon-embossed grains, which as a whole were used for a relatively short span of time. There is certainly much more work to be done in this area than the amount of attention I have given them here.

Part 3: Notes on Grains

My research into cloth finishing provided evidence about two different methods for creating a moiré pattern. Both are traditional calendering processes that have been documented as early as the mid-1700s. Both methods were also used to create moiré patterned bookcloth. To distinguish between them I have named the grain patterns "true moiré" and "engraved moiré." By eye, the appearance is so similar as to be almost indistinguishable, but their significance to the evolution of early bookcloth — both are among the earliest cloth grains in existence — provides ample argument for attempting to identify them. True moiré grain was created by the random intersections of two ribbed surfaces (see note 10). The smooth rollers of a calender machine compressed two layers of cloth, ribbed surfaces face to face, thus creating a "watered" effect. Engraved moiré, on the other hand, employed the use of an engraved roller with "a shallow indenture or engraving cut in it."[46] The bookcloth was thereby embossed with a very precisely engraved design that often so perfectly mimics the moiré effect that it can be difficult to distinguish between them. True moiré grain, when examined through a loupe, is characterized by an unbroken rib, unvaried in width, but along its length it might appear narrow, "faceted," or completely flattened, where the

---

46   *The Modern Dictionary of Arts and Sciences; or Complete System of Literature* (London, 1774), 303.

Illus. 3: Note the small burin slips in this ribbon-embossed grain (as6, here shown enlarged 450 percent)

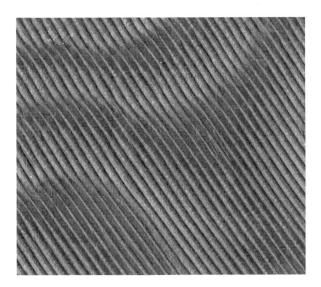

Illus. 4: Note how the engraved lines change from thick to thin, as well as the small marks where the burin slipped (mo12, here shown enlarged 450 percent)

ribbed surface of the top piece was crushed down against the ribs of the bottom piece. By contrast, an engraved moiré pattern will reveal a line created by the engraver's burin that varies in width from thick to thin. The engraving is sometimes so accurate that a small slip of the burin may be the only telling detail, as shown in this detail (Illus. 4).[47]

Both engraved moiré and true moiré peaked in the mid-1830s and dwindled in number by the mid-1840s. In *Binding Variants* Carter illustrates what appears to be a true moiré grain but, curiously, lists two Winterbottom patterns, LR and PR, as equivalents.[48] Forty years later, Gaskell echoed Carter, stating that LR and PR were "irregular moiré pattern(s) introduced in 1831."[49] However, Tomlinson correctly points out that both are actually "whorl" patterns, and did not appear in the Winterbottom catalogue until after 1891.[50] The moiré pattern illustrated in Tanselle (102bd) and Sadleir (viii), and the one in the *BAL*, (AA) depict two variations of a stylized moire, contour moiré (moi4), which appears from 1850 to 1876, with a peak period around 1858. A second moiré-type pattern, snail-trail (moi3), has sharply delineated dates of use: 1847 to 1857. Like the leather patterns, engraved moiré is a large family of patterns that exists in an uncounted number of variations. My work in this area has resulted in breaking down a very broad family into several distinct trends. Continued study will further refine this large family of grains as individual engraved moiré patterns are isolated and associated with a limited range of dates. Later versions of engraved moiré patterns will surely be located that correspond to the Winterbottom patterns RW, AA, and QW from 1892.[51]

Rib grain bookcloth was used throughout the nineteenth century and is by far the largest grain family, but some variations of rib grain can be closely linked to a limited range of dates. Ultra fine rib (rib1) with 24 ribs/cm is specific to the mid-1840s and coarse rib (rib4), with a count

---

47   It has been suggested that other methods of creating a moiré pattern might exist, including a two-step process where the bookcloth is first given a rib grain, and then the moiré pattern is added by means of a roller engraved in relief with a moiré design.

48   Carter, xviii.

49   Gaskell, 246.

50   Tomlinson and Masters, 121.

51   Ibid., 122.

of 6.5/cm, has been found only on books after 1860. "Horizontal" does not identify a true grain, but is a modifier suggested by both Tanselle and Gaskell[52] to identify those bindings where the ribbing runs perpendicular to the spine of the book.[53] Diagonal rib grains, by contrast, can be identified as distinct patterns because the ribbing crosses the weave of the cloth at a 45-degree angle, indicating that the rollers themselves were engraved with diagonal ribs. One type of diagonal rib in common use in the 1870s and 1880s—Winterbottom's "S" grain (rib10)—has a count of 24 ribs/cm. By comparison, ultra fine diagonal rib (rib6, rib5) is an early grain specific to the 1840s and exists in two versions, one with 21 ribs/cm and the other with 33 ribs/cm. Acute diagonal rib (rib9), among the earliest cloth grains, was used between 1832 and 1837.

Like rib, diaper-grain bookcloth is a large family with measurable characteristics that make it possible to isolate those patterns that possess a unique quality and link them to a focused range of dates. Most of the diaper grains were created on a right angle grid (plus or minus 5° to allow for some possible distortion), but several others have distinctly oblique shapes.[54] For example, diamond diaper (dia7) was used on books between 1836 and 1841, and is characterized by elongated diamond shapes. Sadleir, Tanselle, and Ball illustrate coarse diaper (dia4), the earliest diaper grain. Medium diaper (dia3) has 8–9 squares/cm, which is in agreement with medium diaper illustrated by Carter and Gaskell, but is somewhat finer than 6/cm suggested by Ball. Fine diaper (dia2) measures 10–15/cm, much finer than 9/cm suggested by Ball.[55]

The limitations of photographic reproduction have caused confusion about some of the finest textured grains. Sadleir illustrates two separate grains, dotted-line-ribbed and fine dotted-line-ribbed, but the difference between the two patterns appears negligible, as each measures 8 rows/cm.[56] It appears as if one of the illustrations shows the pattern

52   Tanselle, 78. Gaskell, 239. Both authors also use the terms *diagonal* and *moiré* as modifiers.

53   A true horizontal rib grain, if one exists, would be created from a roller engraved with ribs that run parallel to the leading edge of the cloth as it is fed through the machine.

54   Diaper grains are measured along the side of the square or diamond shapes.

55   Ball, 125.

56   Sadleir, *XIX Century Fiction*, plate 31.

running horizontally, and the other vertically. That pattern appears in the CBG as dotted line (net6).

Descriptive names, by nature subjective, can also add to the confusion surrounding certain grain patterns. For example, the *Bibliography of American Literature* illustrates Winterbottom's CM grain and that image was subsequently reproduced by Tanselle, who gave it the designation "408c, coarse sand."[57] Both images are high contrast and depict a coarse granular pattern. Fortunately, a swatch of CM grain bookcloth is included among the "feeler samples" in *Bookcloth, 1823 to 1980*, and it is evident that the grain is composed of long winding strands. Tomlinson recounts that Winterbottom registered CM in 1906, and he considers it a sand pattern that "clearly depicts the ripples left behind in the sand after the tide has gone out."[58] Regardless of the interpretation, the unreliable reproduction does not accurately depict the pattern. CM grain has not been found on a nineteenth-century book in the collection at the Library Company, but it has been included in the catalogue for the sake of completeness.

Unlike the large, but easily quantifiable, grain families like rib and diaper, the leather, sand, and pebble grains have foiled many attempts to sort them. This family of grains appears throughout the nineteenth century in an almost endless series of variations. Ball's study of the various leather, sand, and pebble grains remains the clearest rationale for distinguishing among them.[59] His classifications have been followed as closely as possible in the CBG, and a careful reading of the guidelines set out by Ball is highly recommended for anyone attempting to sort them. Eventually those leather grains that possess a distinguishing pattern or feature will be identified and dates established for their use. Until that time, each of Ball's categories has been illustrated with a range of photographs so that some of the many variations in this large family of grains can be accounted for.

The CBG appears on the pages following this article. A table, arranged by pattern family, lists the cloth grains: fifty-seven new ones, marked with an asterisk, and also the fifty-nine grains previously illustrated by Sadleir, Carter, the *BAL*, Tanselle, Gaskell, and Ball. I have

57 Tanselle, 100.

58 Tomlinson and Masters, 121.

59 Ball, 126–9.

retained the commonly used descriptive name, and instances where an earlier name was changed by a subsequent author have been noted in the table. The third column of the table shows the number of examples and a date range as represented in the Database of Nineteenth-century Cloth Bindings. (Where "eu" appears, that particular grain pattern was not found on an American imprint.) Following the table, a complete set of high-resolution and uniformly scaled reference photographs for each grain will enable positive identification.

Certainly, the very long, and still expanding, list of ribbon-embossed patterns requires a great deal more attention than the space I can give them here allows. Similarly, the strength and focus of this study is primarily early nineteenth-century bookcloth on American imprints. The area of late nineteenth-century bookcloth grains, notably the Winterbottom patterns, on British and foreign imprints are less completely represented here. Much more work remains to be done, and as the study of nineteenth-century bookbinding progresses, I hope the CBG will be seen as a useful reference that provides a consistent set of standards for identifying individual cloth grain patterns and their dates of use. Its presence on the World Wide Web will enable it to be universally accessed to support research in the field of nineteenth-century book studies, and as a reference it will continue to grow as research and data-gathering projects continue both here and abroad.[60]

---

60   The entire Catalogue of Nineteenth-century Bookcloth Grains as well as the Database of Nineteenth-century Cloth Bindings will be accessible via a link from the Library Company of Philadelphia's homepage: www. librarycompany.org.

APPENDIX I

Table of Nineteenth-century Bookcloth Grains

	Grain Description	No. of Examples and Date Range	Ball	Winterb.	Tanselle	Gaskell	BAL	Carter	Sadleir
	Bands								
Ban1	*Dash-and-line	(8) 1832–45							
Ban2	*Thick-and-thin	(3) 1840–1							
Ban3	*Dotted chevron	(1) 1850							
Ban4	Stepped wave	(4) 1854–7	1						
Ban5	Diagonal dot-and-ribbon	(11) 1856–78		EW	112ae	89	PD		
Ban6	Diagonal beaded line	(4) 1858–65		BK		95		(j) wide bead	
Ban7	Dot-and-line	(4) 1862–6		PW	110	88	HT	(l)	fig. xvii
Ban8	*Fine dotted ribbon	(6) 1871–5		MW					
Ban9	*Dot-and-dash	(13) 1870–80							
Ban10	*Fine dash-and-line	(1) 1880							
	Beads[61]								
Bea1	*Dot	(3) 1835–6							
Bea2	Ultra fine bead (15/cm)	(4) 1869–71			202b		BF		fig. x (16/cm)

61   *Bead* grains are measured along the closely packed "strings" at an angle to the edge of the board.

APPENDIX I — *continued*

	Grain Description	No. of Examples and Date Range	Ball	Winterb.	Tanselle	Gaskell	BAL	Carter	Sadleir
Bea3	*Early fine bead (12/cm)	(2) 1839, 1842							
Bea4	*Late fine bead (12/cm)	(1) 1869							
Bea5	Bead (6–7/cm)	(98) 1845–77		D	202	94	BD	(i) close bead	fig. ix
Bea6	*Giant bead (4/cm)	(3) 1857–8							
	Diapers and Diamonds [62]								
Dia1	*Ultra fine diaper (20–22/cm)	(3) 1839							
Dia2	Fine diaper (10–15/cm)	(69) 1836–65			124b		H		fig. iii
Dia3	Medium diaper (8–9/cm)	(19) 1835–51						(d) diaper	
Dia4	Coarse diaper (4/cm)	(15) 1833–5			124c				fig. iv
Dia5	*Smooth diaper (80°, 4/cm)	(4) 1832–6							

62   Diaper and Diamond grains are measured against a scale placed along the side of the shapes, at an angle to the edge of the board

APPENDIX 1 — *continued*

	Grain Description	No. of Examples and Date Range	Ball	Winterb.	Tanselle	Gaskell	BAL	Carter	Sadleir
Dia6	*5.5 diaper (83°, 5.5/cm)	(2) 1835, 1837							
Dia7	*Diamond diaper (55°–65°, 5–6/cm)	(6) 1836–41							
Dia8	*Triple line diamond	(1) 1838							
Dia9	*Ribbed diamond	(4) 1838–53							
Dia10	*Ribbed diaper	(1) 1842							
Dia11	*Ribbed double line diamond	(2) 1845, 1852							
Dia12	*Dotted line diaper	(1) 1866							
Dia13	Double line diaper	(2) 1880, 1882	2						
Dia14	*Wavy diaper	(1) 1846							
	Hexagonal								
Hex1	Fine hexagon	(17) 1852–65	4				HC		
Hex2	Honeycomb	(12) 1852–71			208	97	Z		fig. xxii
Hex3	Hexagon	(2) 1862, 1866			206	96			fig. xxiv
Hex4	Dotted hexagon	(4) 1862–6	3	OW					
Hex5	Pansy	(7) 1864–70			210	98	RH		fig. xxiii

APPENDIX I — *continued*

Grain Description	No. of Examples and Date Range	Ball	Winterb.	Tanselle	Gaskell	BAL	Carter	Sadleir
Leather textures								
Lea1 Morocco	(70) 1833–72 peak 1833–48			402	102	LI		fig ii, coarse morocco
Lea2 Fine ribbed morocco (11–13 ribs/cm)	(9) 1844–60							
Lea3 Ribbed morocco (8–9 ribs/cm)	(79) 1833–66				103b			
Lea4 Stylized ribbed morocco	(3) 1843, 1846, 1857							
Lea5 Horizontal ribbed morocco	(1) 1857							
Lea6 Fine straight grain morocco (11–14 grains/cm)	(37) 1831–54			404b		LG		
Lea7 Straight grain morocco (5–10 grains/cm)	(26) 1841–69			404	103a	L		
Lea8 Cord (8–9 ribs/cm)	(126) 1843–61			306		A		

APPENDIX I — *continued*

	Grain Description	No. of Examples and Date Range	Ball	Winterb.	Tanselle	Gaskell	BAL	Carter	Sadleir
Lea9	Coarse cord (6–7 ribs/cm)	(22) 1852–60			306c		AR		
Lea10	Fine parallel cord (11/cm)	(19) 1856–66							
Lea11	Parallel cord (8/cm)	(20) 1854–66							
	Miscellaneous								
Mis1	*Vermiform	(13) 1833–48							
Mis2	*Small triangles (5/cm)	(1) 1834							
Mis3	*Large triangles (1.5/cm)	(1) 1835							
Mis4	*Crosses	(5) 1835–8							
Mis5	*Early scallop tile	(8) 1835–41							
Mis6	*Continuous string	(1) 1836							
Mis7	*Square tile	(1) 1844							
Mis8	Trefoil leaf	(8) 1856–8	7						
Mis9	Cross and circle	(1) 1860	5						
Mis10	*Diamonds and dots	(1) 1875							
Mis11	*Brick	(1) 1835							

APPENDIX I — *continued*

	Grain Description	No. of Examples and Date Range	Ball	Winterb.	Tanselle	Gaskell	BAL	Carter	Sadleir
	Moirés								
Moi1	True moiré	(15) 1829–46						(c) watered	
Moi2	*Engraved moiré	(21) 1832–50							
Moi3	*Snail trail	(12) 1847–62							
Moi4	*Contour moiré	(19) 1850–76 peak 1858–60			102bd		AA		fig. viii
	Nets and Meshes								
Net1	*Square mesh	(1) 1839							
Net2	*Diagonal mesh[63]	(eu 1) 1841							
Net3	*Lozenge net	(9) 1843–7							
Net4	Net (7–7.5/cm)[64]	(36) 1844–59 peak 1849–53				90			fig. xix
Net5	Coarse net (5–6.5/cm)	(9) 1844–9			118		TB		
Net6	Dotted line	(36) 1865–78		O	108, 108c	87	FL		fig. xv fig. xvi

63 Five grain patterns on the table below have been identified on non-American imprints. These have been identified as "eu," followed by the number of examples.

64 Net and Coarse net are measured along the length of the dash shapes.

APPENDIX I — *continued*

	Grain Description	No. of Examples and Date Range	Ball	Winterb.	Tanselle	Gaskell	BAL	Carter	Sadleir
Net7	Crisscross	(1) 1867			120	91			fig. xviii, fine dotted diaper
Net8	*Square grid	(1) 1869							
Ribs									
Rib1	*Ultra fine rib (24/cm)	(11) 1842–50							
Rib2	*Fine rib (14–17/cm)	(530) 1832–65 peak 1840s–50s							
Rib3	Rib (10–13/cm)	(147) 1836–64 peak 1830s–40s		T	102	84	T	(f) bold rib'd	
Rib4	*Coarse rib (6.5/cm)	(2) 1860							
Rib5	*Ultra fine diagonal rib (33/cm)[65]	(12) 1843–9							
Rib6	*Ultra fine diagonal rib (21/cm)	(2) 1844							
Rib7	Fine diagonal rib (16–17/cm)	(8) 1846–50		GG-18/cm					

65   Diagonal rib grains are measured against a scale placed perpendicular to the ribs, at an angle to the edge of the board.

APPENDIX I — *continued*

Grain Description	No. of Examples and Date Range	Ball	Winterb.	Tanselle	Gaskell	BAL	Carter	Sadleir
Rib8 *Diagonal rib (10–11/cm)	(25) 1832–52							
Rib9 *Acute diagonal rib (10–11/cm)[66]	(9) 1832–7							
Rib10 "S" grain (24/cm)	(107) 1855–98 peak 1876–80		S	102be		S		fig. vii
Ripples								
Rip1 Ripple[67]	(17) 1848–65 peak 1849–50			104	85			fig. xiv, fine ripple
Rip2 *Small compound ripple	(14) 1850–6							
Rip3 *Large compound ripple	(2) 1848, 1849							
Rip4 *Staggered ripple	(3) 1850–2							
Rip5 *Small interlocked ripple	(7) 1850–3							
Rip6 *Large interlocked ripple	(1) 1865							

66 The ribs cross the weave of the cloth at a 35° angle.

67 A variation has crests that are slightly less curved, creating a flatter effect. A photograph of this variation is included in the catalogue.

APPENDIX I — *continued*

	Grain Description	No. of Examples and Date Range	Ball	Winterb.	Tanselle	Gaskell	BAL	Carter	Sadleir
	Sand, Pebble, Bubble								
San1	Sand	(199) 1850–69			408	105		(k)	fig. v
San2	*Sand and stars	(8) 1868–72							
San3	*Sand and triangles	(3) 1868–9							
San4	Patterned sand	(1) 1933		C	410	99	C		fig. vi
San5	Pebble	(58) 1850–80			402b fine morocco 406	106	P	(b)	fig. i, morocco fig. xxi
San6	Bubble	(16) 1859–78			204	107			fig. xii
	Waves								
Wav1	*Feathered wave	(9) 1835–45							
Wav2	*Acute diagonal wave	(5) 1838–50							
Wav3	Diagonal wave	(57) 1847–67 peak 1855–7			106 ae		TZ	(g) ripple grain	fig. xiii, ripple grain
Wav4	Fine wave (9/cm)	(eu 3) 1863–7			106				fig. xi, wavy grain
Wav5	Wave (6–7/cm)	(21) 1847–67 peak 1863–5				86		(h)	

APPENDIX I — *continued*

	Grain Description	No. of Examples and Date Range	Ball	Winterb.	Tanselle	Gaskell	BAL	Carter	Sadleir
Wav6	Coarse wave (5/cm)	(3) 1860					TR		
Wav7	*Zig–zag	(eu 1) 1874							
	Weaves and Checkerboards								
Wea1	*Early checkerboard	(1) 1837							
Wea2	Weave	(1) 1845			116				fig. xx
Wea3	*Right angle weave	(eu 1) 1853							
Wea4	*Open weave	(5) 1870–5							
Wea5	*Coarse open weave	(1) 1877							
Wea6	Coarse checkerboard[68]	(Gaskell) 1890				92			
	Winterbottom[69]								
Win1	Checkerboard	(1) 1924		WJ	122		EC		
Win2	Frond	(eu 1) 1885		CW		109			

68 This grain has not been found on any book in our collection. The image in the CBG was reproduced from Gaskell, fig. 92. In his table of equivalences Gaskell equates this grain with Tanselle's fig. 122, though the two patterns are very dissimilar. In the CBG, Tanselle's fig. 122 has been included among the positively identified Winterbottom patterns as WJ.

69 Five of the Winterbottom patterns listed below have only been found on books printed after 1899. They have been included in the CBG because they appear in other reference works.

APPENDIX I — *continued*

	Grain Description	No. of Examples and Date Range	Ball	Winterb.	Tanselle	Gaskell	BAL	Carter	Sadleir
Win3	Scallop tile	(1) 1887	6	PP					
Win4	Crocodile	(1) 1891		TW		104			
Win5	Lizard skin			LS					
Win6	Crackle	(eu 1) 1895		SW		108			
Win7	Whorl			PR	412		PR		
Win8	Whorl			LR					
Win9	Coarse sand (vermiform)	(1) 1928		CM	408c		CM		
Win10	Coarse linen	(1) 1923		YR	304c				
Win11	Linen	(1) c.1910		AR	304	101a	B		
Win12	Calico	(1) 1915		R	302	100a	V		
Win13	CC	(1) 1885		CC					
Win14	L	(2) 1890		L					
Win15	RR	(1) 1887		RR					

APPENDIX 2
Catalogue of Nineteenth-century Bookcloth Grains [70]

BANDS

Ban1: Dash-and-line (horizontal)

Ban2: Thick-and-thin

Ban3: Dotted chevron

Ban4: Stepped wave

Ban5: Diagonal dot-and-ribbon

Ban6: Diagonal beaded line

Ban7: Dot-and-line

Ban8: Fine dotted ribbon

Ban9: Dot-and-dash

Ban10: Fine dash-and-line

70   All grains are reproduced at actual size. In order to highlight details, some are accompanied by swatches enlarged by 200 percent. A few fine-textured or smooth-surfaced patterns are reproduced in black and white in order to better show the pattern.

BEADS

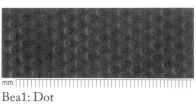
Bea1: Dot

Bea2: Ultra fine bead (15/cm)

Bea3: Early fine bead (12/cm)

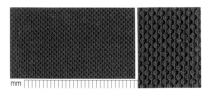
Bea4: Late fine bead (12/cm)

Bea5: Bead (6-7/cm)

Bea6: Giant bead (4/cm)

DIAPERS AND DIAMONDS

Dia1: Ultra fine diaper (20-22/cm)

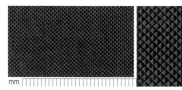
Dia2: Fine diaper (10-15/cm)

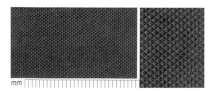
Dia2: Fine diaper (var1) (10-15/cm)

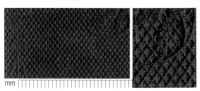
Dia2: Fine diaper (var2) (10-15/cm)

DIAPERS AND DIAMONDS — *continued*

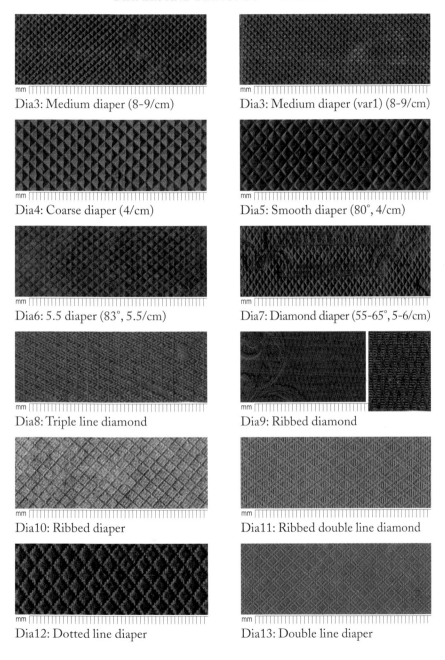

Dia3: Medium diaper (8-9/cm)

Dia3: Medium diaper (var1) (8-9/cm)

Dia4: Coarse diaper (4/cm)

Dia5: Smooth diaper (80°, 4/cm)

Dia6: 5.5 diaper (83°, 5.5/cm)

Dia7: Diamond diaper (55-65°, 5-6/cm)

Dia8: Triple line diamond

Dia9: Ribbed diamond

Dia10: Ribbed diaper

Dia11: Ribbed double line diamond

Dia12: Dotted line diaper

Dia13: Double line diaper

DIAPERS AND DIAMONDS — *continued*

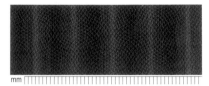
Dia14: Wavy diaper

HEXAGONAL

Hex1: Fine hexagon

Hex2: Honeycomb

Hex3: Hexagon

Hex4: Dotted hexagon

Hex5: Pansy

LEATHER TEXTURES

Lea1: Morocco

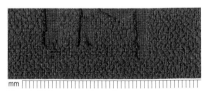
Lea1: Morocco (var1)

LEATHER TEXTURES — *continued*

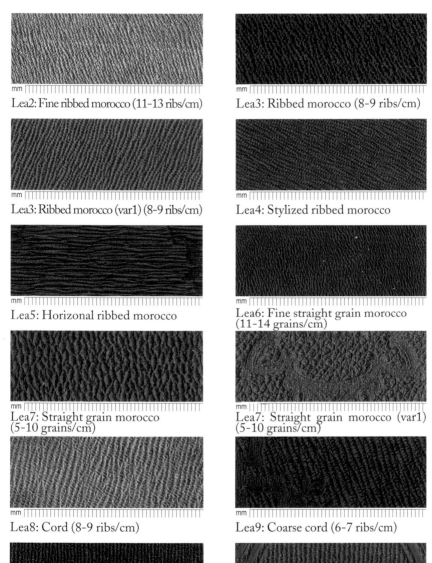

Lea2: Fine ribbed morocco (11-13 ribs/cm)

Lea3: Ribbed morocco (8-9 ribs/cm)

Lea3: Ribbed morocco (var1) (8-9 ribs/cm)

Lea4: Stylized ribbed morocco

Lea5: Horizonal ribbed morocco

Lea6: Fine straight grain morocco (11-14 grains/cm)

Lea7: Straight grain morocco (5-10 grains/cm)

Lea7: Straight grain morocco (var1) (5-10 grains/cm)

Lea8: Cord (8-9 ribs/cm)

Lea9: Coarse cord (6-7 ribs/cm)

Lea10: Fine parallel cord (11/cm)

Lea11: Parallel cord (8/cm)

MISCELLANEOUS

Mis1: Vermiform

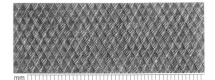

Mis2: Small triangles (5/cm)

Mis3: Large triangles (1.5/cm)

Mis4: Crosses

Mis5: Early scallop tile

Mis6: Continuous string

Mis7: Square tile

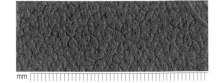

Mis8: Trefoil leaf

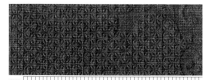

Mis9: Cross and circle

Mis10: Diamonds and dots

Mis11: Brick

MOIRÉ

Moi1: True moiré

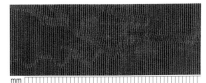

Moi2: Engraved moiré

Moi3: Snail trail

Moi3: Snail trail (var1)

Moi4: Contour moiré

NETS AND MESHES

Net1: Square mesh

Net2: Diagonal mesh

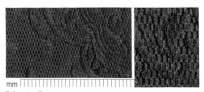

Net3: Lozenge net

Net4: Net (7-7.5/cm)

NETS AND MESHES — *continued*

Net5: Coarse net (5-6.5/cm)

Net6: Dotted line

Net7: Crisscross

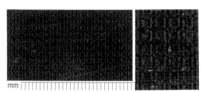

Net8: Square grid

RIBS

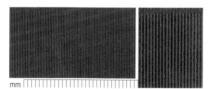

Rib1: Ultra fine rib (24/cm)

Rib2: Fine rib (14-17/cm)

Rib3: Rib (10-13/cm)

Rib4: Coarse rib (6.5/cm)

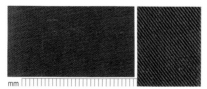

Rib5: Ultra fine diagonal rib (33/cm)

Rib6: Ultra fine diagonal rib (21/cm)

RIBS — *continued*

Rib7: Fine diagonal rib (16-17/cm)

Rib8: Diagonal rib (10-11/cm)

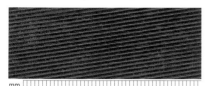

Rib9: Acute diagonal rib (10-11/cm)

Rib10: "S" grain (24/cm)

RIPPLES

Rip1: Ripple

Rip1: Ripple (var1)

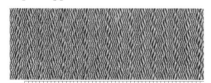

Rip2: Small compound ripple

Rip3: Large compound ripple

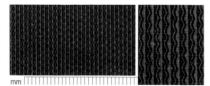

Rip4: Staggered ripple

Rip5: Small interlocked ripple

RIPPLES — *continued*

Rip6: Large interlocked ripple

SAND, PEBBLE, BUBBLE

San1: Sand

San2: Sand and stars

San3: Sand and triangle

San4: Patterned sand

San5: Pebble

San5: Pebble (var1)

San5: Pebble (var2)

San6: Bubble

SAND, PEBBLE, BUBBLE — *continued*

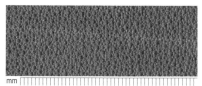

San6: Bubble (var1)

WAVES

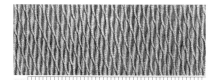

Wav1: Feathered wave

Wav2: Acute diagonal wave

Wav3: Diagonal wave

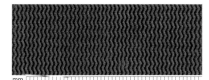

Wav4: Fine wave (9/cm)

Wav5: Wave (6-7/cm)

Wav6: Coarse wave (5/cm)

Wav7: Zig-zag

WEAVES AND CHECKBOARDS

Wea1: Early Checkboard

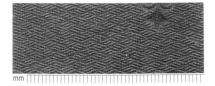

Wea2: Weave

Wea3: Right angle weave

Wea4: Open Weave

Wea5: Coarse open weave

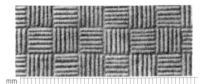

Wea6: Coarse checkerboard

WINTERBOTTOM

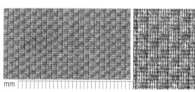

Win1: Checkerboard

Win2: Frond

Win3: Scallop tile

Win4: Crocodile

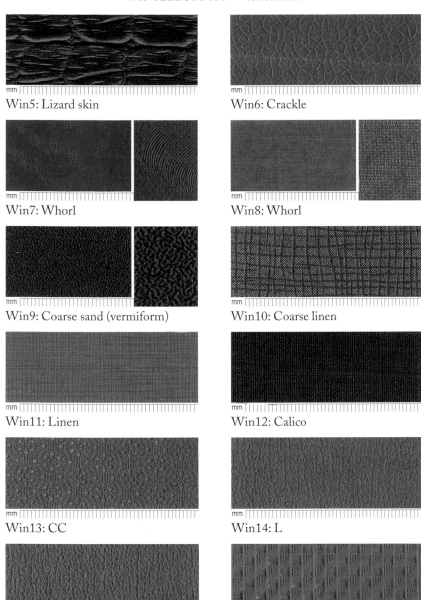

Win5: Lizard skin

Win6: Crackle

Win7: Whorl

Win8: Whorl

Win9: Coarse sand (vermiform)

Win10: Coarse linen

Win11: Linen

Win12: Calico

Win13: CC

Win14: L

Win14: L (inverted)

Win15: RR

Appendix 3
Catalogue of Nineteenth-century Ribbon-embossed Bookcloth[71]

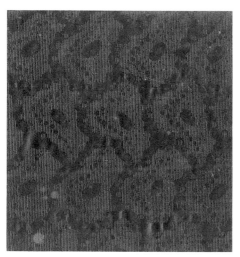

As1: 1835, 1837 (2)

As2: 1832 (1)

71 All ribbon-embossed patterns are reproduced actual size. As = abstract smooth, At = abstract textured, Fs = floral smooth, Ft = floral textured, Gs = geometric smooth, Gt = geometric textured. A few fine-textured or smooth-surfaced patterns are reproduced in black and white in order to better show the pattern.

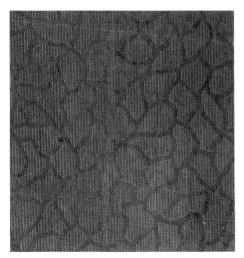

As3: 1831–47 (5)

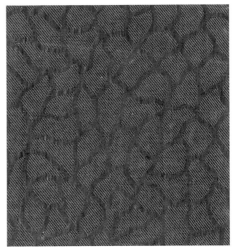

As4: 1835–9 (3) variation of As3, diagonal rib

As5: c. 1832 (1)

As6: 1837–41 (5)

As7: 1835 (1)

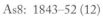

As8: 1843–52 (12)

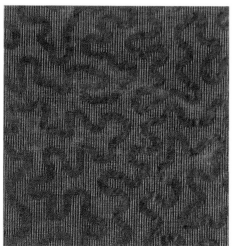

As9: 1838 (1)

As10: 1836 (1)

As11: 1849 (1)

As12: 1820 (1)

As13: 1838 (1)

As14: 1819 (1)

As15: 1833 (1eu)

At1: 1835, 1838 (2)

At2: 1836–9 (4)

At3: 1835 (1)

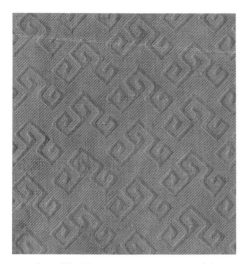

At4: Binding not contemporary (1)

At5: 1837–9 (3)

At6: 1839 (1)

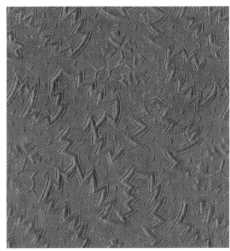

At7: 1832–9 (8)

At8: 1834 (1)

At9: 1836–8 (4)

At10: 1838 (2) depicts various seashells

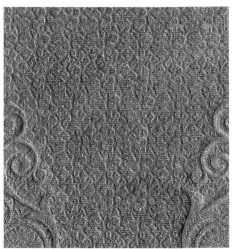

At11: 1840 (1)

At12: 1832 (1)

At13: 1849 (1)

At14: 1849 (1)

At15: 1841 (1)

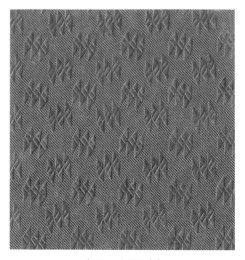

At16: 1836 (1)

At17: 1835 (1)

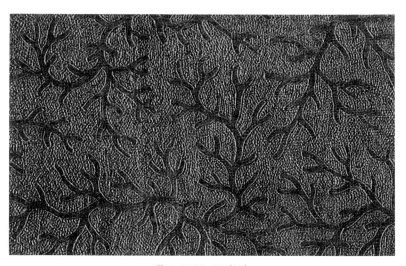

Fs1: 1833–43 (27)

Fs2: 1836, 1838 (2)

Fs3: 1836–8 (4)

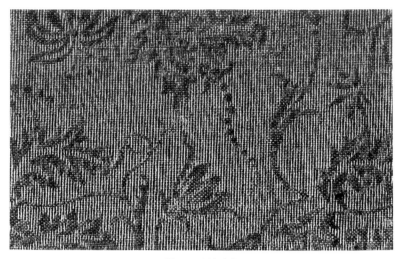

Fs4: 1837 (1)

Fs5: 1834–7 (5)

Fs6: 1834, 1837 (2)

Fs7: 1835–6 (4)

Fs8: 1838 (1) variation of Fs7

Fs9: 1836–8 (6)

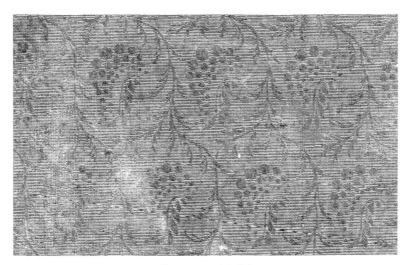

Fs10: 1835–7 (3)

Fs11: 1839 (1)

Fs12: 1840–5 (3)

Fs13: 1838–40 (4)

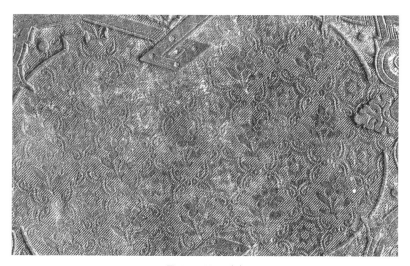

Fs14: 1844 (1)

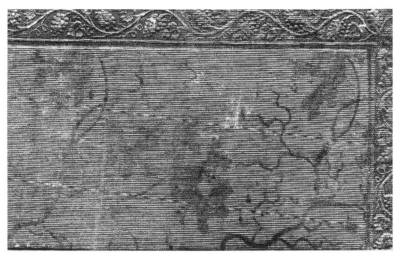

Fs15: 1835 (1)

Fs16: 1837 (1)

Fs17: 1837 (1)

Fs18: 1833 (1) variation of Fs3, horizontal rib

Fs19: 1837 (1)

Fs20: c. 1850 (1eu)

Ft1: 1836–41 (11)

Ft2: 1831–40 (9)

Ft3: 1837–45 (5)

Ft4: 1838 (1)

Ft5: 1837–8 (4)

Ft6: 1839 (1)

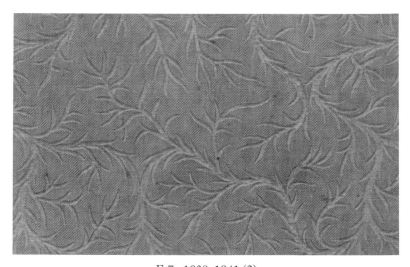

Ft7: 1839, 1841 (2)

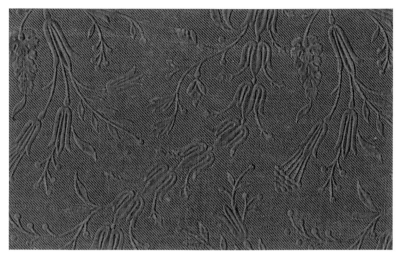

Ft8: 1839 (2)

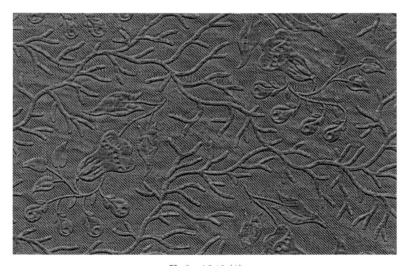

Ft 9: 1840 (1)

Ft10: 1839 (1)

Ft11: 1839 (3)

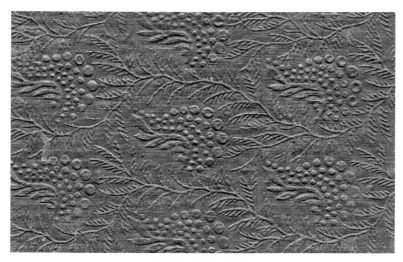

Ft12: 1836–7 (3)

Ft13: 1837 (1)

Ft14: 1845 (1)

Ft15: 1837–9 (4)

Ft16: 1836–7 (3)

Ft17: 1835–40 (4)

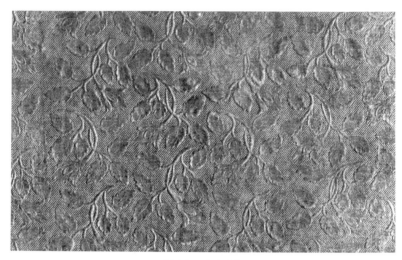

Ft18: 1837 (2)

Ft19: 1838–9 (3)

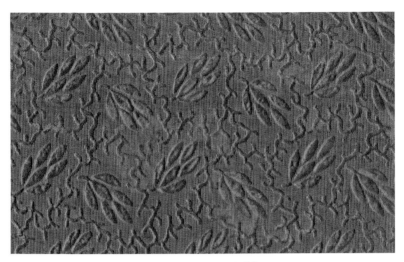

Ft20: 1836, 1837 (2)

Ft21: 1842 (1)

Ft22: 1839 (1)

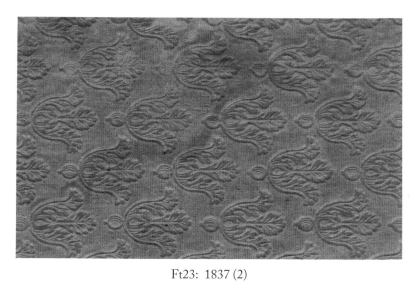

Ft23: 1837 (2)

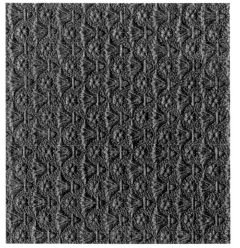

Ft24: 1837–40 (3)

Ft25: 1837 (1)

Ft26: 1837–9 (2)

Ft27: 1834–7 (3)

Ft28: 1837 (1)

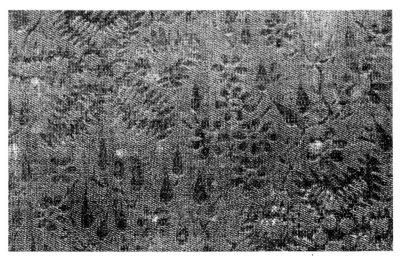

Ft29: 1839 (1)

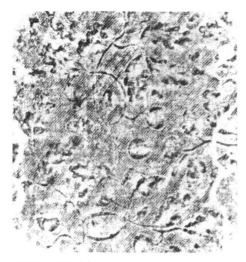

Ft30: 1838 (1) depicts acorns and oak leaves

Ft31: 1837 (1)

Ft32: 1844 (1)

Ft33: 1847 (1)

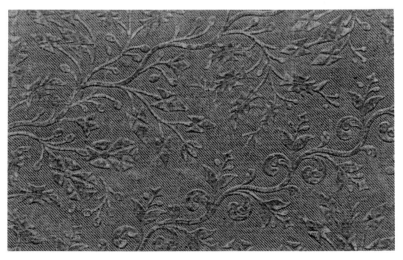

Ft34: 1839 (1)

Ft35: 1838 (1)

Ft36: 1840 (1) depicts cornucopia

Ft37: 1835–7 (4)

Ft38: 1835, 1836 (2)

Ft39: 1839 (1)

Ft40: (1838–40) (5)

Ft41: 1808 (eu1)

Ft42: 1838 (1)

Ft43: binding not contemporary (1)

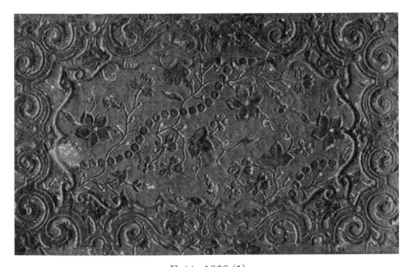

Ft44: 1838 (1)

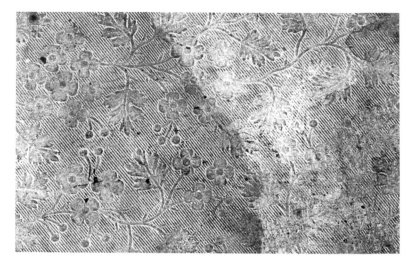

Ft45: 1846 (1)

Ft46: 1840 (1)

Ft47: 1835 (1)

Ft48: 1836 (1) variation of Ft16, diagonal rib

Ft49: 1851, 1856 (2)

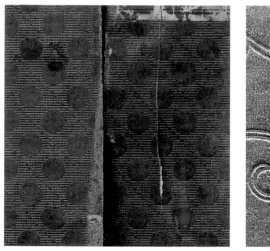

Gs1: 1834 (eu1)

Gs2: 1839 (1)

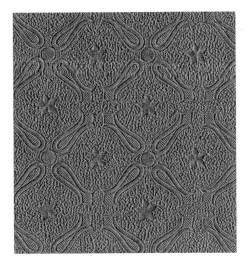

Gs3: 1835 (1)   Gt1: 1831–43 (16)

Gt2: 1838–9 (3)   Gt3: 1835–8 (4)

Gt4: 1837–41 (4)

Gt5: 1837 (1)

Gt6: 1835, 1839 (2)

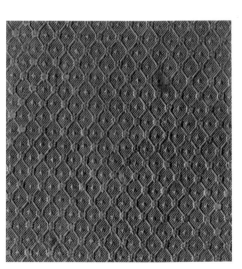

Gt7: 1836–9 (4)

Gt8: c. 1837 (1)

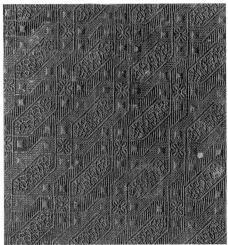

Gt9: 1840 (1)

Gt10: 1844 (1)

Gt11: 1841 (1)

WITHDRAWN
COLORADO SPRINGS, COLORADO

Gt12: 1836–8 (4)

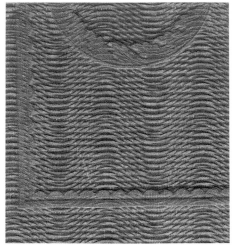

Gt13: 1834, 1836 (2)

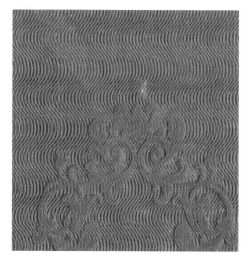

Gt14: 1837 (1)

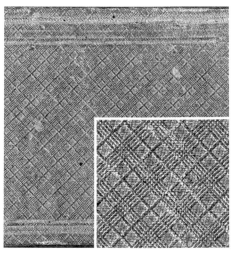

Gt15: 1840 (1) inset enlarged 200%

Gt16: 1844 (1)

Gt17: 1839 (1)

Gt18: 1841 (1)

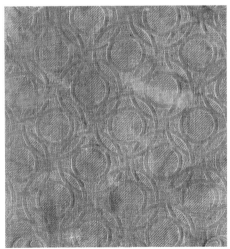

Gt19: 1840 (1)

Gt20: 1845 (1) variation of Gt15,
inset enlarged 200%

Gt21: 1835 (1)

Gt22: 1835 (1)

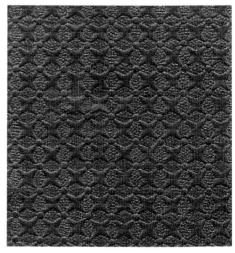

Gt23: 1838 (1) variation of Gt6